TABLE OF CONTENTS

HOW TO USE HOME SCREEN ....

THE QUICK SETTING GUIDELINES 5

DISPLAY GUIDELINES 8

APPS TIPS 9

Just recently, the South Korean tech giant Samsung released the most formidable phone ever built; Samsung Galaxy S10 and S10+. These state of the art phones was released alongside the S10e and S10 5G. From our calculations, the tech giant has 4 phones in the 2019 S10 series.

These ambitious launching has added a complete fresh air on the S10 series. The Android 9 Pie and One UI are an evolution of Samsung Experience UX and TouchWiz.

We have gone through the deepest part of this smartphone to root-out all that you should know.

Let's take a look at a simple S10 search tip that will help you master the phone swiftly.

The best way to find anything on the phone is to swipe down to the quick settings, there is a search button. Enter the search query and your phone will automatically search your settings, contacts, calendar appointments, etc. for a result. The search tool is very useful. Another way to use the search query is to simply launch the apps tray and tap the finder bar.

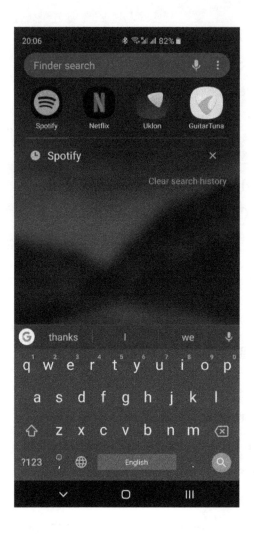

How to use Home screen

On the Home screen of these devices display the app shortcuts and widgets. It could be quite tricky if you are using the device for the first time. To have a full grasp of the Home screen, here are basic tips that will help you.

Editing the Home screen – If you press and hold the wallpaper for a while, it will activate the edit option. You can edit the themes, widgets, pages, or even add, and delete the entire Home screen.

Changing the size of the Home screen – Press and hold on the wallpaper for a while and tap the ***Home screen settings*** option will appear. The 4x5 size will help you view everything clearly on your Home screen. You can use either the 4x6, 5x5, or 5x6 setting to cram more in. However, we prefer a 5x6 setting.

Resizing the widgets – To resize your widget, press and hold to select a widget. Then drag the blue box when it appears to resize the widget.

Customizing the navigation bar – Go to ***Settings > Display > Navigation*** bar to alter the arrangement of the buttons.

Removing the navigation bar and using gestures – You can also remove the navigation bar if you choose to. So you don't have to tap on the screen button, rather you can swipe to the location.

Customizing the status bar – Go to ***Settings > Notifications> Status*** bar to view the available options. Limiting the notification icon to 3 or using all is possible. The battery percentage icon can also be turned on or off.

Landscape view – This option is put off on the default. So to turn it on, go to ***Settings > Home screen > Portrait mode only***. It will allow you to view the Home screen in landscape.

Creating a folder – Drag app on another on the Home screen to create a folder. If you want to delete the folder, Open folder > Press and hold app > Tap remove an app. You can also add an app to the folder by dragging it into the folder or tap the ***Add apps*** button.

Changing the colour or renaming a folder – Open a folder and input the name of your choice. You can change the colour of the folder by tapping the dot on the right side. Pick the colour you want.

Delete a folder – Press and hold the folder and tap the *Remove from home* button.

Go to Bixby Home – Bixby Home puts together all the information it gathers from other parts of the phone such as location or the social feed, weather, etc. Swipe to the right side to view the Bixby Home.

Turning off the Bixby Home – Press and hold the wallpaper > Swipe to the right > Bixby Home panel will display > Tap the off button.

Changing the Home screen – For more flexibility on your Home screen, you can download an app known as Nova. Go to the Play Store to download and install. Tap *Settings > Apps > Press the menu tab at the topmost right > Tap default apps > Home screen > Select a launcher of your choice*.

View app suggestions – If you press the Recent apps tab, a thumbnail of all your recent app pages will display. A line of suggested apps will also appear based on what the phone believes you will like to use. To turn this function off, press *Recent apps > Tap the menu on the right side > Turn off the Show suggested apps*.

Popping out conversation in a different window – If you are used to Facebook, you will have noticed the Facebook Chat Heads. The Galaxy S10 can also pop-out a conversation into a floating button. Go to **Settings > Advanced features > Smart pop-up view**.

The quick setting guidelines

This part of the Samsung Galaxy S10 allows you to access the most used settings for your phones such as Wi-Fi, Bluetooth, and power saving modes. It's a collection of shortcuts. You can access this by swiping down from the topmost part of the screen.

How to instantly access the quick setting and notifications pane on your Home screen - Swipe down from any part of the screen and the notification pane will slide down. When you swipe down again quick settings will appear. This feature is really helpful on the Galaxy S10. You will have to press and hold the wallpaper because it is off by default. Tap the **Home screen setting > Quick open notification panel**.

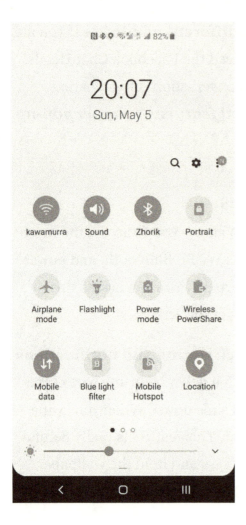

Edit quick settings - If you want to change the shortcuts, swipe down twice to view the full grid. To open the menu, tap the 3 dots and tap Button order. The full list of options will appear across the pages. If you want to reorder or delete a shortcut, simply drag.

Top tip: The first six apps are displayed in the compact view across the top of the screen. For easy access, just make them your first settings shortcuts.

How to change the quick settings grid size - If you want to change the density of the quick settings icons, simply press the *Menu button > Tap the Buttons grid > Tap 5x3* to get a lot more on to one page.

How to access device settings from quick setting - This tip is very useful if you want to access settings instantly. Just press and hold the shortcut and it will instantly take you to the full settings menu. It's helpful if you want to access Wi-Fi, Bluetooth, or power saving options.

Display guidelines

These two phones are built with a display function know as Infinity-O display. It is among the best mobile displays you can find around. The Infinity-O display gives you room to carry out several visual functions including cutting-out the front camera.

These tips will give you a broader sense of what your device can do.

Hiding the front camera - Assuming you don't want to use the front camera, you can hide it in a dark banner. Go to *Settings > Display > Full-screen apps*.

How to switch the Settings menu dark with night mode - If you prefer a darker look, go to *Settings > Display > Night mode*.

How to alter the display colours - Go to *Settings > Screen mode* to change the outlook of your display. The default settings of the display colour are natural. You can choose an option to make the colour vivid, change the colour temperature, or the RGB settings.

Altering the display resolution - The default setting of the display resolution is **Full HD+**. However, you can change it to

Quad HD+ if you choose. To use the display resolution of your choice go to **Settings > Display > Screen resolution**. If you use a display resolution that is lower, your battery will last longer.

How to switch on the video enhancer - This feature is somehow hidden. You really have to dig deep to discover this option. However, reading this has definitely made it easier. This feature works with apps like Netflix, Play Movies, YouTube, etc. Go to **Settings > Advanced features > then Video Enhancer**. You can either switch it on or off if you choose.

Using the Blue Light Filter - This option alters the colour of the display to reduce the blue light, avoid straining your eye and provide better sleep. Go to **Settings > Display > Blue light filter** to alter the times and strength of the effect.

One-handed mode - For a tall individual, it may be easier to use the Galaxy S10+ in one-handed mode. This feature will allow you to swipe in diagonal angles either from left, right, up, down. Go to **Settings > Advanced features > One-handed mode > Just hit the Home button thrice** and it will shrink to One-handed mode. Upon activation of the One-handed mode, you can switch to left or right when tapping the arrows.

Apps tips

Do you know that your apps tray can be customized? As you keep reading, you will discover how to customize the Galaxy S10 and S10+. Below are very useful tips that will help you enjoy your device;

Display all apps on the Home screen - This option is used by most people. To remove the apps try, press and hold the *Home screen > Tap Home screen settings > Home screen layout > Tap Home screen only or Home screen and Apps screen*.

Force – close apps - Tap on the app switcher button to see the apps you used recently. To close an app, swipe up on the preview. This feature is not available on an iOS device. You can't swipe on multiple apps at the same time. You can also find a close button across the bottom of the screen.

Split screen apps - If you love using more than one app at the same time, go to the Multitasking view. Look for any of the apps you want to use the split-screen mode. Tap the app's icon, then hit the Open in split-screen view tab. The first app will go to the top of the screen pending when you launch the second app.

Add or delete an apps tray button - Usually, the default settings of the device don't have an apps tray button. However, if you want an apps tray to go to the *Home screen settings > Tap apps button*. You can put it on or off.

How to show or hide your apps tray - Like you already know, the Galaxy S10 allows you to view the apps tray by simply swiping up. To return to the home page, all you have to do is swipe up and the apps tray will disappear.

Changing your apps screen grid size - You can also change the density of the apps on the apps tray or page. To do this, go to *Settings > Tap apps screen grid > 5x6*.

Alphabetize your apps - *Tap menu on the apps tray > Press the menus at the top right side > then tap Sort*. This will allow you to use the alphabetical order. Just press that option and the whole thing fall into place.

Reorder apps - To access this option, tap the **Menu button at the top right side > Hit the Sort button > Select custom order**. This will allow you to drag the apps to your desired position.

Creating apps tray folder - You can create a folder for your apps whether the apps are arranged alphabetically or in custom mode. To do this *press and hold an App icon > Drag it over another app* > a folder will be created automatically. If you choose, you can change the name and colour of the folder.

How to use Finder to search your entire device - You can locate a Finder option at the top of the apps screen. It will allow you to search contents in your app too. You can search for Feedly, Play Music, Messages, Reminder, Calendar, and other apps with this option. *Tap the Finder bar > Press the Menu button at the right of the apps tray > Press Manage apps > Select where you want to search*.

Manage the apps found by the Finder - Assuming after conducting a search through Finder and it returns information that you don't need, you can put off some of the apps it can access. Press the *Menu at the top right of the apps tray > Tap Finder settings > then Manage apps.* You can turn off the apps here.

How Finder's app suggestion works - As soon as you tap the Finder at the top of the apps tray, it will provide app suggestions based on apps you used recently. To cancel this, *Go to Finder settings > Tap show suggested apps turn this feature off or on*.

Uninstall apps - You do this directly from the app icon. *Press and hold the app for a while > A pop-up menu will display > Tap the uninstall app*. You can uninstall some apps, but for a core app you can only disable it.

How to add apps to your Home screen - *Press and hold the app shortcut on the apps tray > Drag it to the top of the page*. Alternatively, select Add to home when the menus pop-up.

Digital Wellbeing - Google's Digital Wellbeing initiative is growing faster than the Android maker's own Pixel device. *Tap Settings > Tap Digital Wellbeing* to enable or customize the stats tracker to assist you to reduce the amount of time you spend staring at your device.

Apps Management

To avoid adding app icons to your Home screen just go Home screen setting (then hold and press the wallpaper, the Home screen settings will appear), tap Add apps to Home screen. Switch this option off so that it doesn't automatically create shortcuts to all the apps you install on your Home screen.

How to set a default app - If you have more than one app carrying out the same function on your device, you can choose which will be your default app. Simply tap *Settings > press the Menu button at the right-hand side > hit Default apps*. You will see all the apps that you have chosen as your "default app".

Controlling your app permissions - You can manage all permissions for all your apps individually with the Android Pie. Head to *Settings > Apps > choose the App you want > tap Permissions*. This option will allow you to switch on and off the permissions. For instance, you can turn off or on Location or Contacts access.

Lock screen and always-on display

The lock screen appears when the phone is locked. The lock screen has two parts. One appears when *Always-on display* is turned on. This option will let you view some information. The other is the main lock screen. You can't access any information here. These options are very important on the Galaxy S10 because of the in-display fingerprint feature.

Turn on always on display - If you want to turn on this option, Go to *Settings > Display > Lock screen > Tap always on display*. This will display when the phone is on standby mode. You can use schedule to program when it will appear either all times or when you press your phone.

How to change the always-on click style - The S10 provides various types of always-on display. To change the always-on clock style, Go to *Settings > Lock screen > Clock style*. This option also allows you to change the clock for always-on display and the lock screen. You can also change the colours too.

How to add a piece of music or FaceWidgets to the phone lock screen or always-on display - FaceWidgets are referred to other information on the lock screen or always-on display. Most often a music controller is turned on by default. If you don't want it, go to *Settings > Lock screen > FaceWidgets*. You will see the entire options to put on or switch off the Bixby Routines, weather condition, etc.

Steps to alter the brightness of Always-on display - The always-on display is linked to the brightness settings on your device automatically. If you want to set it manually, go to *Settings > Lock screen > Always-on display > Auto brightness*. Turn off the "Auto brightness" yourself to do it manually.

Changing the lock screen shortcuts - If you want to access your apps quickly, you can set up two shortcuts on the lock screen. This works for just the lock screen and not for the always-on display. Here is how to access the option, go to *Settings > Lock screen > App shortcuts*. You can either use the left or right shortcut. Switch it off too is at your discretion.

Disable or enable the lock screen notifications - You can disable or enable notifications on your lock screen. Go to *Settings*

> *Lock screen > Notifications*. This option will let you hide contents, display app icons or deactivate notifications. To ensure that all the notifications with contents to appear don't choose *Hide*. You can hide contents for some apps and not all.

How to alter the appearance of the lock screen notifications - Apart from being able to alter the information that shows on the lock screen, you can also change the appearance. To choose this option, go to *Settings > Lock screen > Notifications*, to alter the transparency of the lock screen notifications. The text will stand out better if you invert it against the background.

How to hide the lock screen notifications - Assuming you don't want lock screen notifications from some apps, go to *Settings > Apps > a list apps will appear > Press the app you want*. For example, if you tap WhatsApp, choose Notifications. All the notifications that control WhatsApp will appear. Just hit the Whatsapp notifications and lock screen. You can also switch off the lock screen notifications too.

How to display a roaming clock on the lock screen - This is one of the best options on this device. This feature turns on automatically to your local time. A roaming clock can display the home time zone. Here's how to go about it, *Settings > Lock screen > Roaming clock*. You can also adjust the position of the home time zone.

Security and unlocking features

One of the notable changes on the Samsung Galaxy S10 is the inclusion of an ultrasonic in-display fingerprint scanner.

Security tip: If the biometrics don't work, the device reverts to using your PIN or password. So this simply means that biometrics is not guaranteed security. So it is advisable to use a very strong PIN or password. If anyone who attempts to access your device via the PIN or password security, will find it difficult. Kindly note that biometrics are not used as security per se but for convenience.

How to activate fingerprint or face security - If you want to activate the fingerprint or face security, go to *Settings > Biometrics and security*. This option allows you to set up a face or fingerprint recognition. You will also have to set up a PIN or password as alternative security.

Note: If you choose fingerprint security, register with each finger on both hands so that you can unlock your phone with whichever finger you choose.

How to display the fingerprint scanner - To have the fingerprint icon display, you have to tap the screen of your device. Go to *Settings > Biometrics and security > Fingerprints > Insert PIN or password* > then toggle *Show icon when the screen is off*.

Instant lock - The standby button immediately locks the phone when you press it. Go to *Settings > Lock screen > Secure lock settings* to lock the phone whenever the phone goes to sleep or you press the standby button. To set the time when the phone will sleep, you will find plenty of time options.

Smart Lock or Bluetooth unlock - To activate or disable this option, tap *Settings > Lock screen > Smart Lock*. This feature is found in most Android devices. You can choose a device you trust that can unlock your phone when it is connected to it. Some of such devices are like the smartwatch or your car.

Important tip: You can use this option on Samsung One UI to return to stock Android visuals.

How to wipe the phone automatically - To guard against bad guys having access to your device or cracking it, you can wipe it automatically. Go to *Settings > Lock screen > Secure lock settings*. You can auto factory reset the device if 15 attempts are made to unlock your phone.

Locking network and security functions - This option simply entails that your network configuration cannot be altered when the device is locked. This will help you find your phone in case it gets stolen. That notwithstanding, it simply means that you have to unlock your device to activate flight mode. Go *to Settings > Lock screen and security > Secure lock settings > select the turn on or off button*.

Encrypting your Memory card - This security option will protect your SD card from any tampering if it is removed out of the phone. When you encrypt the SD card, it can only be read by your phone. Go to **_Settings > Biometrics and security > Encrypt Memory card_** to activate this option.

How to save your personal documents and apps in a safe folder - You don't have to be worried about people accessing your mobile device and viewing files that they have no business looking at. You simply opt for a Secure folder. This will definitely guarantee another layer of security. You can add files, images, videos, and so on to the folder. If you don't certain apps to be accessed too, you can add them to this folder. **_Go to Settings > Biometrics and security > Secure folder_**.

Notification guidelines

The more complex the device, the more notifications you will receive. The good thing about this phone is that it provides you with constant information. So it is left to you to choose which notifications are important to you. Before now we discussed about the lock screen section. So you can scroll back to take a look.

Snooze alerts - If you don't want to alerts to disrupt the use of your device, you can snooze some alerts. Swipe the alert to any direction of your choice until a settings icon and a bell appears. Press the bell and choose the time you want to snooze the alert for.

How to switch off app notifications - Head to **_Settings > Notifications > Hit See all_** to get an easy toggle option for the apps on your device. If you choose, you can switch them off or choose the type of notifications that will display.

Display app icon badges - This feature is new to Android phones. The Icon badge will display the notification that each app on your phone has. Go to **Settings > Notifications > App icon badges**. Here you can switch off the notifications of the individual app.

How to view app notifications - The fastest way to view your app notifications is to simply press and hold an app shortcut. This feature is advanced and an extension of icon badges. As soon as you press and hold an app that is displaying the badge sign, you will be able to view the notifications. Go to **Settings > Notifications > App icon badges** (it's at the bottom of the page directly beneath "Show notifications"). This works on the Home screen, so it is advised to use it for your favourite apps.

How to disable a notification - This feature is found on most Android devices and it's very important. Assuming you receive a notification from an app that you don't want to ever see again, swipe the notification to view the Setting.

Volume controls, sound, Do Not Disturb controls

Understanding and mastering the Do Not Disturb feature on this phone is important you need to master. A proper understanding will help you to receive notifications when you want it or silence your phone but still receive the important notifications. The Samsung Galaxy S10 has 5 volume sliders. Are you surprised? The sliders are for ringtone, audios or videos, all notification, system, Bixby voice.

How to snub the media volume toggle - To choose this option Swipe lower volume or tap *Settings > Sounds and Vibration*. Ordinarily, this option is off as default. After activating it, pressing the volume button will make just the media volume to move. If it is not activated, it will control ringer volume and switch to media when a media file is playing on your phone.

Accessing the volume settings - If you press the up or down volume button, the volume you want to change will display. However, if you choose, you can swipe down the banner to access the 5 sliders.

Altering the vibration levels for everything - To change the amount of vibration you will receive for everything, go to *Settings > Sounds and Vibration > Vibration intensity*. Choose the level of vibration you want for calls, notifications, and touch.

Switching to vibration alerts - If you want the phone to be in silence mode but prefer vibration alerts, press the speaker icon on the pop-up. It will automatically switch to vibration. You can also press and hold down the down button until it slides down to the vibration mode.

Activating the silent mode - When you press and hold down the down button, it takes the phone to the vibration but not silent. If you want the silent mode activated, go to *Settings > press the Sound shortcut*. Don't forget to switch the sound back on, or you might lose important notifications, calls, messages, etc.

How to switch off the charging, unlocking, and keyboard sound alert - One thing about this device is that it will beep on every action you take. Whether you touch the keyboard, receive a message or plug in your charger. To change this feature, go *to Settings > Sound and vibration > System sounds and vibration*. You will find all the options to turn all these features off.

Enabling and controlling Dolby Atmos - The Samsung Galaxy S10 speakers are AKG and it has a Dolby Atmos option. To alter the settings, Go to *Settings > Sounds and vibration > Sound quality and effects*. You can change the Dolby Atmos feature to auto, movie, music or voice. You can also switch on the Dolby Atmos option while playing games with your device.

How to customize the sound of the phone - Some S10 users are not aware this option is available. To access it, go to *Settings > Sounds and vibration > Sound quality and effect > Adapt sound*. You can use a profile feature or you can customize the option to suit you.

Using the Do Not Disturb option - The Do Not Disturb option allows you to silence your phone with some exceptions. To access the option, Swipe down to Quick setting and press the Do Not Disturb button to switch it on. You can also program it to function at a scheduled time. For example, when you are the office or at night. To view the complete menu, press and hold the Quick settings.

How to set alarms and exceptions in the Do Not Disturb - This option is perfect if you want to silence. However, if you want to some notifications, then you can choose the notifications that will form part of the exceptions. Go *to Settings > Sound and vibrations > Do Not Disturb > Allow exceptions*. You can set the exceptions to allow alarms or other notifications as exceptions.

How to set notifications in Do Not Disturb - Although you can silent sounds and vibration on this option, you can also do the same to notifications. Go to *Settings > Sound and vibration > Do Not disturb > Hide notifications*. In this option, you can switch off the icon badges, notifications, pop-ups and status bar icons.

How to set an app to ignore the Do Not Disturb feature - When you turn on the exceptions, it will allow you to get some apps to get notifications when the Do Not Disturb option is activated. For instance, the Do Not Disturb is switched on but you also prefer the Ring Video Doorbell to still come through. To activate this feature, go to *Settings > Apps > select an App > tap Notifications > view the notifications that the app offers > press the type of notification >scroll to the bottom of the list > press "Ignore Do Not Disturb" > switch it on*.

Tips and tricks to use the camera and photo

The camera of the Samsung Galaxy S10 is a little bit similar to that of S9+. It has a wider angle lens. However, they are a lot of new features that the S10 camera comes with. Below are tricks and tips that will help you get the best out of the camera.

How to switch on the suggestion mode - This feature is new. What it does is to analyze the environment and recommend the best view. It will recommend the best shot and also assist in lining up the shot with the help of a guide. *Launch camera > press Setting at the top > shot suggestion mode*.

How to use Scene optimizer to enhance images - This feature makes use of AI to enhance photos and also allows longer handheld night photos. In the viewfinder in the camera app, there you will find a swirly icon. If the blue scene optimiser is switched on, it will identify the scene and select the best settings. Assuming the swirly icon doesn't appear, go to *Camera setting > and toggle on scene optimiser*.

How to activate the Quick Launch - Tap the Standby button twice to open the camera. You can open the camera from the screen or any part of the phone. Go to *Camera app > Settings > toggle "quick launch"* if this feature is not turned on. You can also open the camera through the lock screen.

How to switch camera modes - To switch the camera mode, you can swipe across the camera display to move from one mode to another.

Editing camera modes - You can choose any camera modes of your choice, add or remove. Go to *Settings > Camera mode >*

Edit mode > pick the modes of your choice. You can decide to open your device camera to use the most recent mode.

How to use Instagram mode - This phone has a bespoke Instagram mode in the camera app. The Instagram mode is one of the modes that you can use to take pictures. As soon as you take the picture, it will be ready for posting on Instagram.

How to quickly move from rear to front camera - If you look closely, you will find a button between the front and rear camera. However, you can also switch with just a swipe. You simply swipe up or down the display to switch from one camera to another. Another option is to press and hold the power and the cameras will switch.

Activate raw capture - To save a file as DNG and JPEG file at the same time, go to *Settings > Save options*. Select the option to save both files at the same time. If you must use this feature, you need to activate the Pro mode. Simply switch on the Pro mode to save raw files.

How to use video stabilization - To use this feature with the rear camera, go to *Settings and scroll down, you will find Video stabilisation*. Tap it to activate.

Capture in HDR10+video - The HDR10+ is a beta feature, but it lets you take video in HDR. Go to *Video mode > open camera setting > Advanced recording functions*.

How to take a selfie portrait - This is the hottest part of this phone. It's very helpful if you can get someone who can take a good picture of you. Simply switch to the front camera and tap the selfie focus and pout. You can try out 4 different effects.

How to identify an object with the use of Bixby Vision - The camera app shows Bixby vision at the top left corner > press Bixby and it will attempt to identify an object. You can also use apps for AR.

Using the AR Emoji - You will find this option at the top of the camera across the Bixby Vision. It will allow you to capture an emoji that looks like you or use an AR character. Press AR emoji to use this feature.

How to shoot a long exposure image - Open the camera app and swipe across > pick Pro > tap on the option to change the length of exposure (it's at the right-hand corner) > Select the length of time. The exposure compensation icon will let you know if you have gone past the exposure limit.

How to Switch the Aperture yourself - The dual aperture option changes automatically from f/1.5 and f/2.4. This will depend on the shooting condition. You can do it manually if the camera is in Pro mode. Launch the camera and switch to pro mode. All the settings including shutter speed will appear. The aperture option will also appear at the left in a bubble. Just tap it to switch from f/1.5 to f/2.4.

How to alter the gallery view - If you want the image on your phone to appear smaller or bigger, pinch on the screen to zoom and it will change the thumbnail view.

How to take shots with a Google Camera port

Although it has a single rear camera, Google Pixel 3 is perceived by a lot of people to have the best camera on any smartphone. The fascinating qualities of the Google Pixel camera are as a result of Google's incredible camera software. The Google camera app makes use of Google's industry-leading techniques. The Samsung S10 and S10+ can also use the port to take beautiful images. Although the port has Google Pixel's Night Sight, HDR+ and Portrait Mode, the S10 wide angle lens will work with it.

Google Camera is a very useful app. In fact, it is considered by many as one of the most important apps for an Android device. Using it with the Samsung Galaxy S10 series is mind-blowing. This app is the first of its kind that works with a Night Sight, HDR+, Portrait Mode, and a wide – range mode on the Snapdragon Galaxy S10 series.

How to install a Google Camera port on the Snapdragon S10, S10e, or S10+?

If you want the wide angle lens on your Samsung Galaxy to work, then you have to do the following;

1. Download the current Google Camera APK
   (https://www.androidfilehost.com/?fid=1995089523397913303).

2. Install the APK on your Snapdragon Samsung Galaxy S10 or S10+.

3. Download config files for saved settings (https://www.androidfilehost.com/?fid=1395089523397913302).

4. Extract the config files to the root storage with the file path /Internal Storage/GCam/Configs/.

5. Launch the app and tap the black area close to the shutter button twice.

6. Pick option s10csMar2.xml.

7. Select Restore.

8. Enjoy using Google Camera!

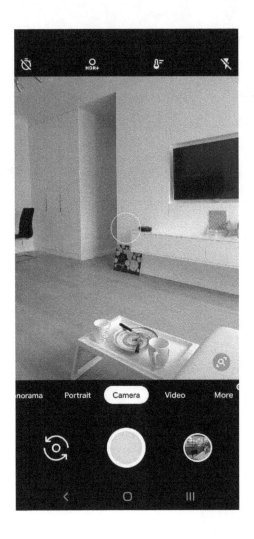

Screenshot tips and tricks

Taking a screenshot with your phone - Press the volume down and standby buttons at once. It will capture a screenshot.

Palm swipe for a screenshot - Another way to take a screenshot is via a swipe. Go to **Settings > Advanced feature > Motion and Gesture > switch on Palm swipe to capture.**

How to use smart capture - You have a lot of options to play around with for screenshots on your Samsung Galaxy S10 phone. To use smart capture, go to *Settings > Advanced features > Motions and gestures > Smart Capture*. You can use this feature to capture a full website page.

Smart select is an edge panel, it's possible to swipe into it via the edged screen. Here is how;

Go to *Settings > Display > Edge screen > Edge panels*. This menu will help you activate edge screen first and smart select edge panel too.

Go to the page you want to capture.

Swipe through the edge panel and select the smart select.

Select the shape or type of selection you like. You will find a rectangle, circle, pin to screen or create a gif option.

After making the selection, you will be returned to the capture page. You can alter the size of the frame and tap done when you are through. If you want to create a gif, tap record and tap stop when are through.

What you captured will display and an option to share, save or extract will appear. Select whichever one you want.

How to capture a gif from the screen - Creating a gif is very easy with this device. It allows you to create a gif instantly from any media playing on your device. For instance via YouTube or

Instagram. Switch on the smart select edge > Swipe to smart select from the edge > Pick animation. A preview window will show on your screen and it will allow record video to create a gif.

Tips to master edge screen

The introduction of the Infinity display is a good one by Samsung. You can also choose to switch it on or off.

How to switch off the edged screen - Go to *Settings > Display > Edge Screen > toggle off edge panels*.

Managing an edge screen content - The S10 and S10+ have edge functions. To activate it go to *Settings > Display > Edge screen to manage edge panels*.

How to add or remove edge panels - Go to *Settings > Display > Edge screen > press the edge panels. Simply select a panel, then add or remove the panel you want*.

How to move the edge panel handle to any position - You can reposition the edge handle to anywhere from the left or to the right screen. Press and hold, then drag it to any position you want. If you want the edge panel handle to remain static, read the settings below.

How to alter the size and transparency of the edge panel handle - Go to *Settings > Display > Edge screen > Edge panels*. Press the menu on the top right-hand side and choose *Edge panel handle*. This setting will let you change the handle and also the make it invisible, change the colour, size and add vibration when you touch it.

Activate edge lighting for notifications - Go to ***Settings > Display > Edge Screen > then tap Edge lighting***. You can alter the pattern of the edge lighting and select the apps you want it to notify you about. It works with any app.

How to manage digital assistants

This device has two digital assistants namely Bixby and Google. However, Bixby is Samsung's customized digital assistant. You can also install another digital assistant like Alexa if you choose. Here is how to manage all your digital assistants;

Google Assistant – Press and hold virtual the on-screen home button to open the Google Assistant. You can start up a conversation with Google. Don't forget, this works with your Google account and the set-up.

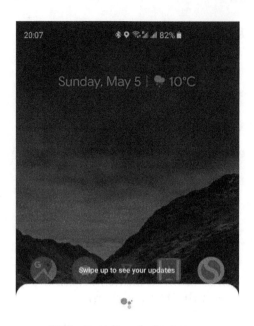

Accessing Google Assistant after deleting the on-screen buttons – To access the Google Assistant with gestures, *Swipe and hold the bottom middle of the display > the Google Assistant will display > Press OK* to start using it.

Disabling the Google Assistant – To remove the Google Assistant from the home button shortcut, go to *Settings > Apps > Tap the top right-hand menu > Press the Default apps >*

select the None option. This will disable the Google Assistant on the Home screen.

Changing your digital assistant – For instance, if you download and install another digital assistant like Alexa, you can set it as the default assistant app. As soon as that is done, you can access Alexa on your home instead of any other assistant.

Reassigning the Bixby button- The Bixby button is located at the left side of the S10. It can perform other functions than just opening the Bixby. You can also set it to launch another app. Tap the *Settings button > Advanced feature > Bixy key*.

Turning off Bixby Voice wake-up and listening – This option will only work if you have set-up Bixby before. If you haven't, then Bixby will not work. Open *Bixby > Tap the top right of the menu > Press setting > pick the "never" option* for Bixby listening to you and tap turn off to stop the voice wake up.

Tips and tricks for Bixby

Bixby is an assistant on this device. It was launched in 2017 and it debuted on the Samsung Galaxy S8. Since then, it has appeared in other models of Samsung. This AI assistant can also carry out several functions too. However, it is broken down into Bixby Voice, Bixby Home and Bixby Vision.

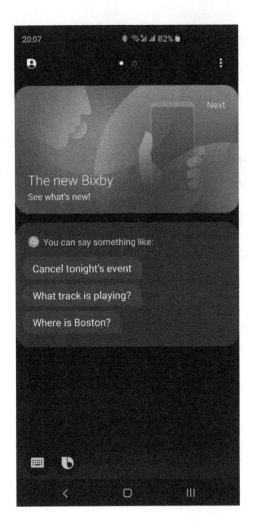

How to switch off Bixby Home - This topic was discussed previously, but if you don't need a Bixby Home press and hold the wallpaper > the Home screen controls will appear > Swipe to the right > the Bixby Home panel will show. There is a toggle button on the top right side of the screen. You can switch off the Bixby Home panel if you don't want it.

How to customize the content of Bixby Home - This assistant fills itself with unnecessary information, but you can select what information it should absorb. Launch Bixby Home > tap the menu at the right-hand side of the screen > hit Cards > the list of apps that can feed into Bixby Home. You can also switch off any feature you don't need.

Setting up a Bixby Routine - Go to *Settings > Advanced features > Bixby Routines.* This option will allow you set-up routines that will serve as a reminder when you travel out of the country.

How to designate a button to Bixby - When you tap the Bixby button, it activates the Bixby Voice and also aids you to access the associated screens. These screens are almost like Bixby Home but the difference is that they are separately handled. You can alter the function of the Bixby button. Go to *Setting > Advanced function > Bixby key*. To carry out this change, you have to sign into Bixby. You have an option to reassign another app to the Bixby button. Simply note that you can't stop the button from activating Bixby but rather add an extra function.

How to activate or deactivate a Bixby's voice - You can use Bixby hands-free, but you have to set it up. *Tap Menu at the right side to access settings > locate Voice wake-up > choose whether to wake up the phone with Bixby*.

Blocking Bixby Voice - You can switch Bixby Voice if you choose. This will entail that Bixby will not be able to locate your voice. Go to *Bixby Settings > tap Automatic listening > pick Never*.

How to use Bixby to access Settings on your device - One of the interesting qualities of Bixby is that you can access your phone Settings through it. To do this, ***press and hold Bixby key > say a word or what you want > say what you want to change on your device***.

How to use quick commands to alter the functions of your phone - You can use quick commands will let you use Bixby Voice in a jiffy. Tap the ***Bixby button > tap Menu > tap Quick commands.*** It will let you set up what you want when you say something.

How to get Bixby to respond when it's connected to a Bluetooth device - This option is very interesting. ***Go to Bixby settings > Voice response > Look for an option that lets Bixby only respond with voice when connected to a Bluetooth device***. It's good for a hands-off control, especially when you are driving.

Using Bixby Vision to translate - Launch the camera and Bixby Vision will appear at the top left side of the screen > press it to open Vision > at the far left bottom you will find Translate > point it at whatever you want it to translate.

Battery tips

These tips will help you use your phone battery properly. Although the S10 battery is long lasting, these tips will help it stay longer.

Wireless PowerShares - Do you know that Samsung Galaxy can reverse charges wirelessly? The phone has a quick setting toggle for this option. It will let you charge another device if they are placed back to back. Press the button and keep the device you want to charge at the back of the phone. Be it an iPhone or any other device, it will start charging instantly.

Check out what is consuming your battery - Go to **Settings > Device care > press Battery** to view the phone's battery usage for the past 7 days. If you press **Battery usage**, it will display what's eating up your battery.

Activating the power saving mode - You can go to Quick settings and tap the settings or go to *Settings > Device care > Battery*. You can choose either medium or maximum battery saving mode.

Activating fast charging - Simply go to *Settings > Device care > Battery* and press the menu at the top right for extra settings >tap *Fast cable charging*. This will make your phone charge faster.

How to manage app power saving - Go to *Settings > Device maintenance > Battery* > the app power monitor will appear. You can choose apps that the phone will save battery on the background.